First World War
and Army of Occupation
War Diary
France, Belgium and Germany

34 DIVISION
102 Infantry Brigade
Cheshire Regiment
1/7th Battalion.
1 June 1918 - 29 July 1919

WO95/2462/2

The Naval & Military Press Ltd
www.nmarchive.com
Published in association with The National Archives

Published by

The Naval & Military Press Ltd

Unit 10 Ridgewood Industrial Park,

Uckfield, East Sussex,

TN22 5QE England

Tel: +44 (0) 1825 749494

www.naval-military-press.com

www.nmarchive.com

This diary has been reprinted in facsimile from the original. Any imperfections are inevitably reproduced and the quality may fall short of modern type and cartographic standards.

© **Crown Copyright**
Images reproduced by permission of The National Archives, London, England, 2015.

Contents

Document type	Place/Title	Date From	Date To
Heading	34th Division 102nd Infy Bde 1-7th Bn-Cheshire Regt Jun-Dec 1918 1918 June-1919 Jly Form Egypt 53 Divn, 159 Bde.		
War Diary	Palestine Sheet XIV	01/06/1918	05/06/1918
War Diary	Egypt	06/06/1918	30/06/1918
Miscellaneous	1/7th Battalion, The Cheshire Regiment. Summary Of Numbers Reporting Sick Daily, Admission To Hospital, And Changes In Strength, Etc. I Or The Month-Ending 30th June/18	30/06/1918	30/06/1918
War Diary	Belgium & France	01/07/1918	01/07/1918
War Diary	Sheet 19 Bambecque	02/07/1918	06/07/1918
War Diary	L 3 b 9.8	07/07/1918	11/07/1918
War Diary	Belgium & France Sheet 19	12/07/1918	17/07/1918
War Diary	Beauvais Sheet 29	18/07/1918	18/07/1918
War Diary	Soissons Sheet 22	19/07/1918	20/07/1918
War Diary	Oulchy Le Chateau 1/20000	21/07/1918	21/07/1918
War Diary	Fere En Tardenois 1/20,000	22/07/1918	31/07/1918
Miscellaneous	Appendix I		
War Diary	Report On The Operations Ending From 22 July 1918 to 2nd August, 1918		
Miscellaneous	The Following Casualties Were Incurred During The Operations:-	31/07/1918	31/07/1918
Miscellaneous			
War Diary	Oulchy Le Chateau 1/20000 Fere En Tardenois 1/20000	01/08/1918	04/08/1918
War Diary	Belgium and France	05/08/1918	06/08/1918
War Diary	Sheet 27 1/40,000	07/08/1918	16/08/1918
War Diary	Sheet 28 NW	17/08/1918	26/08/1918
War Diary	Sheet 27 NW & 28 NW	27/08/1918	31/08/1918
War Diary	St. Omer (Hazebrouck 5A) Sheet 28 NW 1/20000	01/09/1918	07/09/1918
War Diary	Sheet 28 SW 1/20000	08/09/1918	09/09/1918
War Diary	Sheet 28 SW 1:10000	09/09/1918	23/09/1918
War Diary	Sheet 28 SW SE 1/20000	23/09/1918	01/10/1918
Miscellaneous	Narrative of Operations 1/7th Cheshire Regt. Sept 3rd-5th 1918	08/09/1918	08/09/1918
War Diary	Sheet 28 SE 1/20000	02/10/1918	18/10/1918
War Diary	Sheet 29 1/40000	19/10/1918	31/10/1918
Miscellaneous	1/7th Bn The Echelon Regt.	14/10/1918	14/10/1918
Operation(al) Order(s)	Operation Order No. 19	24/10/1918	24/10/1918
Miscellaneous			
Miscellaneous		27/10/1918	27/10/1918
War Diary	Sheet 29 1/40000	01/11/1918	03/11/1918
War Diary	Sheet 28 1/40000	04/11/1918	14/11/1918
War Diary	Tournai Sheet 1/100000	15/11/1918	30/11/1918
War Diary	Louranai 1/100,000	01/12/1918	14/12/1918
War Diary	NW Europe 1/250000	15/12/1918	31/12/1918
War Diary	Force	08/01/1919	14/01/1919
War Diary	Force	01/01/1919	22/01/1919
War Diary	Beule	23/01/1919	31/01/1919
War Diary	Lohmar	01/02/1919	06/02/1919
War Diary	Siegburg	09/02/1919	28/02/1919

War Diary	Bornheim	01/03/1919	31/03/1919
War Diary	Weingarisgasse	01/07/1919	01/07/1919
War Diary	Weingarisgasse	28/06/1919	28/06/1919
War Diary	Wahn	11/07/1919	29/07/1919

34TH DIVISION
102ND INFY BDE

1-7TH BN CHESHIRE REGT
JUN - ~~DEC 1918~~

1918 JUN — 1919 JLY

FROM EGYPT
53 DIV, 159 BDE

Sheet 1

WAR DIARY
or
INTELLIGENCE SUMMARY
(Erase heading not required.)

Army Form C. 2118.

1/7 Cheshire Regt 102/34

Vol I

June 1 – Dec 18

Place	Date	Hour	Summary of Events and Information	Remarks and references to Appendices
PALESTINE SHEET XIV	1/6/18	06.30	Marched to RAMALLAH & Bivouaced on HAWK HILL The Battn was inspected by C.O. Corps Commander who bid farewell to the Battn on proceeding over seas.	
	2/6/18	06.30	Marched to ENAB Had breakfast about 3 miles from starting point Arrived Bivouac 10.15 Casualties nil	
	3/6/18	06.30	Marched to LATRON Arrived at Bivouac Area at 10.30 Casualties Nil	
		14.00	Cooks tran party left for SURAFEND	
	4/6/18	02.00	Marched to SURAFEND Arrived at 07.00	
	5/6/18		Rested in Bivouac Area	
	6/6/18	3.30	First train entrained at LUDD Station 19.30 2nd train entrained	
EGYPT	7/6/18	04.55	1st train arrived at KANTARA and proceeded to Camp at KILO 5	
		11.30	2nd train arrived	
	8/6/18	06.00	Batt Drill until 12 Apparent bathing in Canal	
	9/6/18		" "	
			Coy Parades	
			" "	
	12/6/18		Interior economy inspection by C.O. 11.00 Gas test Bathing Coy drill	
			Battn entrained 1st June	

Sheet II

Army Form C. 2118.

WAR DIARY
or
INTELLIGENCE SUMMARY.
(Erase heading not required.)

Instructions regarding War Diaries and Intelligence Summaries are contained in F. S. Regs., Part II. and the Staff Manual respectively. Title pages will be prepared in manuscript.

Place	Date	Hour	Summary of Events and Information	Remarks and references to Appendices
EGYPT	25/6/18		Preparing for Entrainment to Port of Embarkation	
	11/9/18		Entrained for Port of Embarkation	
	13/9/18		Marched to onward	
	15/9/18		Sailed overseas	
	22/9/18		Disembarked	
	23/9/18		Entrained at TARANTO, ITALY	
	29/9/18 14.45		arrived at PROVEN and marched to Billets at BAMBECQUE	
			APPENDIX	
			1. Summary of Strength	

H. E. Mouat, Lt. Colonel
Comdg. 1/7 Cheshire Regt.

1/7th Battalion, The Cheshire Regiment.

Summary of numbers reporting sick daily, admissions to hospital, and changes in strength, etc., for the month ending ~~XXXX=XXXXXXX~~.
30th June/18.

Date.	Strength. Offcrs.	Strength. O.R.	Nos. reporting sick.	Nos. Adm. Hosp.	Nos. rejoining from Hosp.	Other Casualties.
1/6/18.	34	903	5	3	5	1 O.R. joined for duty. Lt. Stafford to U.K.
2/6/18.	34	903	3	1	1	
3/6/18.	34	902	6	1	-	
4/6/18.	34	899	16	4	-	1 O.R. from Trade Test.
5/6/18.	34	900	10	1	-	2 " " " "
6/6/18.	34	899	14	1	-	
7/6/18.	34	900	15	-	1	
8/6/18.	33	895	39	1	-	Lt.Lindop & 6 O.Rs. taken off strength. 2 O.R. from Trade Test. 1 O.R. trans. to Gn.Bn. 3 O.R. to Base Depot.
9/6/18.	33	890	21	1	-	
10/6/18.	37	958	12	1	-	Lt.Carswell.) " Power.) Rejoined " Ashcroft.) Bn. 2/Lt.Loakman.) from & 68 O.R.) Hosp. 1 OR.joined Bn.for duty
11/6/18.	37	962	24	2	23	40 OR.returned to Base Depot. 23 OR.rejoined Bn.for duty ex.Base Depot
12/6/18.	37	960	31	2	-	
13/6/18.	37	962	18	1	3	3 OR.posted Bn.for duty.
14/6/18.	37	965	9	1	1	1 OR. -do-
15/6/18.	29	968	10	-	1	1 " from Trade Test. Capt.Winlow.) To No.1 " Casells.) Base " Buckton.) Depot. " Davies.) Surplus Lt.Ashcroft.) to est- " Hanford.) ablish- " Wagstaffe.) ment. 2/Lt.Middleton.) 5 O.R. -"-
16/6/18.	29	963	8	-	-	
17/6/18.	29	962	5	1	-	
18/6/18. to 21/6/18.	29	962	-	-	-	
22/6/18.	29	953	20	9	-	
23/6/18. to 28/6/18.	29	887	81	66	-	
29/6/18.	29	877	20	10+	-	+ Adm. en route from Taranto to Ploven.
30/6/18.	29	877	-	-	-	

WAR DIARY
or
INTELLIGENCE SUMMARY.
(Erase heading not required.)

SHEET 1

7th BATTN. CHESHIRE REGT. Army Form C. 2118.

Vol 2

Place	Date	Hour	Summary of Events and Information	Remarks and references to Appendices
ST OMER	1/7/16		Battn was visited by A 102 Bde 34 Div II Army Corps II Army. Army was absent in Paris	
FRANCE SHEET 10 SQUARE 20C	2/7/16		Clearing up	
			In Corps Reserve	
3/7/16		Inspection of Battn by Corps officer	
	4/7/16		GOC 34 Div accompanied by GOC 102 Bde inspected the Battn. Expressed himself very satisfied with the journey	
	5/7/16		Training under Coy arrangements	
	6/7/16		Training	
	7/7/16			
28.C.9.8	8/7/16		Marched to Scots Camp arrived 12.30 pm CO & Coy Commdts	
			Reconnoitred the Line E. POPERINGHE Defences	
	9/7/16		Training. Hostile Grids reconnoitred Sub sector line E POPERINGHE Defences and Corps Commander	
			Inspected by GOC in C II Army 9.30 pm Battn took over allotted portion of	
	10/7/16		EAST POPERINGHE LINE returned to Camp about 3 am	
	11/7/16		Training under Coy arrangements as per programme	
			Gas mask-inspection Coy arrangements. Honoured gas officer visited the Battn. Awaiting Gas.	

SHEET 2

WAR DIARY
or
INTELLIGENCE SUMMARY.

(Erase heading not required.)

7th Batt'n. Cheshire Regt. Army Form C. 2118.

Place	Date	Hour	Summary of Events and Information	Remarks and references to Appendices
BELGIUM	12/7/18	06.00	All Coy fires on 30' range at School Camp. Also Gunnery under Coy arrangements	Reinforcements [?] B G.O.R
FRANCE SHEET 19 L.3.6.9.c	13/7/18	11.30	Marched from School Camp to PROVEN Stn entrained at 5pm arrived ST OMER 6 pm. Marched CORMETTE CAMP	
	14/7/18	09.00	Musketry on Open rifle range. Coy training remainder of day	
	15/7/18	06.00	Batt'n Drill under Co. Received orders to entrain at 11.30. Marched Pool strength than 2350 prior to follow Reg'l Transport 12.30 by March took to BAM BECQUE Batt'n at 2.55. Marched to ST.OMER & entrained for PROVEN. BRUGGE Quartermaster	
		8.40 pm	Entrained to BAMBECQUE arriving 10pm Couvelier kit	II Corps
	16/7/18	10.20	Entrained at REXPOEDE for destination unknown. Batt'n less 1/2 Coys	
	17/7/18	2.20	The Coys under Capt 7 DEW HARMAN entrained at REXPOEDE for destination unknown	
		20.40	Batt'n less 3 Coy detrained at SURVEILLIERS marched unit Reg't Transport to MONT LOGNON Detrd (About 12 miles) arriving about 4.15 am	
BEAUVAIS SHEET 21	18/7/18	4.15	Batt'n less the 3 Coy arrived at Billeting area MONTLOGNON Casualties Nil	
			The Coy detrained at SURVEILLIERS marched to MONTLOGNON arriving about 11 am	2/Lt W.C. ROBINSON 2/Lt H.T. CLAPHAM 2/Lt F.A. STRINGSEY 2/Lt W.E. NASH
SOISSONS SHEET 22	19/7/18	05.55	Received orders to embus which was completed by 07.00 & proceeded by road to VEZ. Map reference SOISSONS SHEET 22 Sq A. 3. 10. 17	

(A7092). Wt. W1285g/M1293. 75,000. 1/17. D. D. & L., Ltd. Forms/C2118/14.

SHEET 3.   7th BATTN. CHESHIRE REGT.

Army Form C. 2118.

WAR DIARY
or
INTELLIGENCE SUMMARY.

(Erase heading not required.)

Instructions regarding War Diaries and Intelligence
Summaries are contained in F. S. Regs., Part II.
and the Staff Manual respectively. Title pages
will be prepared in manuscript.

Place	Date	Hour	Summary of Events and Information	Remarks and references to Appendices
SOISSONS SHEET 22	20/7/18	11.30 pm	Bn. instructed by G.O.C. 102 Bde.	A/B
		11.50 A	Bn. with Light Transport moved by road to PUISEUX arriving at 4.30 am	A/B
DULCHY LE CHATEAU 1/20.000	21/7/18	—	on 21st July	A/B
		—	an account in previous diary. Officers Reconnoitring Centres sent out to reconnoitre route through forest de RETZ to LONGPOINT	A/B
FERE EN TARDENOIS 1/20.000	22nd	—		
	31st	—	Detailed accounts of the operations during this period are attached herewith	A/B 20 July 2Lt. G. WILLIAMS 2Lt. G. NEATH 2Lt. R. TEDCASTLE 15 D.R.

Sheet 4

WAR DIARY
or
INTELLIGENCE SUMMARY.

7th Batt'n. Cheshire Reg't Army Form C. 2118.

Place	Date	Hour	Summary of Events and Information	Remarks and references to Appendices
			Appendix I. Report of Operations including between 22nd July and 31st 1918	A.I.
			H. L. Knox. Lt Col. Comdg 1/7 Bn The Cheshire Regt.	

REPORT ON THE OPERATIONS EXTENDING FROM 22-July, 1918 to
2nd August, 1918.

Reference Maps: OULCHY LE CHATEAU 1/20,000.
               FERE EN TARDENOIS 1/20,000.

The 102nd Brigade which had been in bivouac at PUISEUX marched through the forest de RETZ to an area N.E. of LONGPOINT arriving there about 4 p.m.

G.O.C. 102nd Bde., Bn. Commanders and Company Commanders met near LONGPOINT at 10 a.m. and proceeded to MONT REMBOUF Farm for the purpose of reconnoitring the line to be taken over from the 38th Regiment of the French Army.

O.C., 1/7th Cheshire Rgt. proceeded alone from this point to PARCY TIGNY to reconnoitre the battalion sector which consisted of the old PARIS Trench Line N.E. and E. of the Village of PARCY TIGNY and a point S.E. of the Village where the Road from PARCY TIGNY to HARTENNES et TAUX cuts the trench line.

At 9 p.m. the 102nd Bde. with the 1/7th Ches.Rgt. the leading battalion moved from rendezvous via Bde. Hd. Qrs. (400+ N.E. of Mont REMBOUF Farm) to PARCY TIGNY and relieved the French.

The battalion relief was completed by 1 a.m. on the 23rd July.

The disposition of the battalion was 2 Companies in the line, 1 in support and 1 in reserve, and Bn. H.Q. in the village of PARCY TIGNY. Communication was maintained with the 2/4th Queen's Regt. 101st Bde. on our right and 1/1st Herefordshire Regt. on our left.

All preparations were made in anticipation of an advance at dawn.

Orders for the advance were received at 6.30 a.m. and the signal for the advance was given at 7.40 a.m.

"A" & "D" Companies advanced through the cornfield to approx: 1,000+ due EAST of the village and 200+ W. of TIGNY COUREMAIN Road.

Considerable opposition was met with from enemy machine guns in the BOIS de REUGNY and from the high ground on our right front. Owing to insufficient support on both flanks the battalion was unable to advance any further and the line was consolidated. The support and reserve Companies were moved up to the old Paris Trench Line. Throughout the day PARCY TIGNY WAS subjected to heavy bursts of enemy shell fire.

Approximate Casualties during the day were 180.

During the night of 23/24th July, "A" & "D" Coy's. which had suffered heavy casualties were relieved in the front line by "B" & "C" Coy's. and withdrew to the Paris Trench Line. Bn. H.Q. was moved from the village to a dugout in the Trench Line.

24th July.

No event of importance occurred during the day. Moderate shelling by both sides and a little sniping by the enemy.

Consolidation of the front line continued.

25th July.

Heavy shelling by our guns during the morning in connection with the French attack on our left.

Between 8 & 9 a.m. our front line was shelled by one of our own batteries.

Defence organised in depth in 4 lines in conjunction with the battalion on our left.

"B" & "C" Companies formed the front line and support, "D" Coy. in support and "A" Coy. in reserve.

Our right flank was slightly advanced and joint Posts established with the 101st Bde. on the boundary Road.

26th July.

No change in the situation. Patrols pushed well forward at least 800+ in front of our line and found enemy M.G.Posts. still in position.

Indications were noted of the withdrawal of enemy guns further eastwards. Also destruction of enemy dumps observed.

27th July-28th July.

Slight enemy shelling during the day. Bn. was relieved by the 38th Regt. of the French Army at about 1.30 a.m. on the 28th July, and marched via BLANZY to BOIS de MADON arriving there at 4.30 a.m.

During the march the main road to BLANZY was heavily shelled, including gas shells.

- 2 -

27/28th July. continued. ....

G.O.C. 102nd Bde. to BILLY SUR OURCQ.

10 p.m. Bde. marched through BOIS de NADON via ST. REMY BLANZY to BOIS de BAILLETTE where it bivouaced and remained in Divisnl. Reserve.

29th July.

8.15.a.m. 1/7th Ches.Rgt. & 1/1st Hereford Rgt. moved forward in support of the Division moving south of BOIS de BAILLETTE thence across the SOISSONS - CHATEAU THIERRY Road in a north-easterly direction. The left of the 1/7th Ches.Rgt. at GRAND ROSOY, the right BOIS de MONTCEAU inclusive. The left of the 1/1st. Hereford Rgt. BOIS de MONTCEAU exclusive and the right HILL 158 S. of BEUGNEUX. Heavy enemy shell fire met with on marching from the cover of the wood and approaching the Soissons Road.

"C" & "A" Coys. crossed the Road and moved forward 300+ halting there for the 1/1st Hereford Rgt. to come up into position.

9.30 a.m. Orders received from 102nd Bde. not to advance any further. O.C. Called to Brigade H.Q. where instructions were received to push forward under cover of BOIS de MONTCEAU to the Paris Trench Line with support lines to be consolidated in BOIS de MONTCEAU. "C" & "A" Companies occupied Paris Trench Line east of BOIS de MONTCEAU and 300+ Northwards towards GRAND ROSOY and obtained touch with the French Division on our left. "B" Company in BOIS de MONTCEAU and "D" Coy. in reserve near the Soissons Railway. "A" Company pushed about 500+ further forward and whilst ordered to push forward at 2.30 p.m. the leading Brigades which had advanced towards BEUGNEUX were found to be retiring and the enemy made strong counter attacks on our left front. The Divisional line withdrew to the old Paris Trench Line and after a stiff struggle the enemy counter-attack was beaten off. During the whole morning all approaches to the front line had been subjected to an intense shell fire and the line itself was heavily bombarded by the enemy.

4. p.m. The enemy Infantry all withdrew N. of GRAND ROSOY - BEUGNEUX ROAD. The woods N. of the Road were occupied by enemy M.Gs. Close touch was maintained with the French at GRAND ROSOY.

The 2/4th Somerset L.I. and the 1/4th Cheshire Regiment had moved up into the neighbourhood of the Paris Trench Line in support.

5.30 p.m. Intense enemy barrage put down on our trench line compelling the French to withdraw on our left. This necessitated our left flank being bent back to prevent the line being enfiladed.

Orders received to push forward 700 N.E. of MONTCEAU WOOD and for patrols to endeavour to work through the wood N. of GRAND ROSOY - BEURNEUX Road.

30th July.

2.30 a.m. Positions advanced to within 300+ of GRAND ROSOY - BEURNEUX Road. 2 Companies in front finding their own supports, Bn.H.Q. in sunken road N.E. of BOIS de MONTCEAU, Reserve Company in Paris Trench Line (Bn. Organised as 3 Companies). The patrols were unable to penetrate the northern woods owing to enemy M.Gs. 1/1st Hereford Rgt moved forward to a position 200+ right of the sunken road. Intense enemy shelling practically all day.

31st July.

4.30 a.m. Very heavy enemy barrage lasting 1 hour. 1/4th Royal Sussex Regt. (101 Bde.) moved up on our left and started consolidating. Our patrols entered 200+ into the big wood N. of the Road and were then held up by enemy M.Gs. Enemy Trench Mortars registered on our front line. Touch was maintained with the 103 Bde. on our right.

The attack of 103 Bde. on HILL 158 with which our patrols were endeavouring to co-operate did not take place. This was not known until some hours afterwards. 1/7th Cheshire Regiment outpost Bn. for 102 Bde.

- 3 -

The following casualties were incurred during the operations:-

OFFICERS.

Killed.
Lt.C.C.Foster. 29/7/18

Wounded.
Lt.H.W.Ives. 23/7/18
Lt.A.G.K.Piggott. 23/7/18
2/Lt.H.J.Clapham. 23/7/18
Lt.J.N.Watson. 23/7/18

Wounded & remaining at duty.
Lt.Col.H.L.Moir. 23/7/18
2/Lt.J.H.Lewis. 23/7/18
2/Lt.R.Teacastle. 29/7/18

Died of wounds.
Capt.T.Furnell.
2/Lt.F.A.Sproson.} Wounded
2/Lt.D.J.Smith. } at 29th July 1918

OTHER RANKS.	K.	W.	M.	Wounded & Remaining at duty.	Gassed.	Shell Shock.	Died of wounds.
	25	197	10	2	21	10	2
			5				

H. L. Moir.
Lieutenant Colonel,
Commanding 1/7th Bn. The Cheshire Regiment.

31/7/18.

NATIONAL
(6424) Wt. 25894/168

WAR DIARY or INTELLIGENCE SUMMARY

Army Form C. 2118.

1/7 Cheshires

Vol 3

Place	Date	Hour	Summary of Events and Information	Remarks and references to Appendices
OULCHY LE CHATEAU 1/20,000	August 1918 1st	—	Bn. became Div Reserve and prepared to move forward in support.	
FERE EN TARDENOIS 1/20,000		9.30 a.m.	Bn. pushed forward & occupied line GRAND ROSOY - HILL 158 and consolidated in U.A.A.	
		1.45 p.m.	Bn. moved up through BEURGNEAUX to a ravine 400 yds N.E. of the village and came under the orders of the 101 Bde. Bn. remained for the night in reserve to the 101 Bde. AAA	
	2nd		During the day Lewis gun Centre was sent forward to assist in clearing the ground.	
			Ravine LE MONTJOUR and Pt 199	
		6.30 p.m.	Bn. came again under the orders of the 102 Bde & marched down to the PARIS Road Line N.E of BOIS de MONT CENU to await bivouack for the night.	
	3rd	—	Bn. remained in Bivouac. Major J.C.L. 34th Div. presented French decorations to Lt. Col. H.L. MOIR, Major R.D. FLUNDER and 3 O.R.'s	
	4th	9 a.m.	Bn. entrained and proceeded to OGNES arriving at 6.30 p.m. where it remained for the night. Time in trains refreshments supplied the Bn. Two	
BELGIUM and FRANCE	5th	—	Bn. remained at rest.	
	6th	8 a.m.	Bn. marched to LES PLESSIERS BELVILLE and entrained at 12 noon	
SHEET 27 1/40,000	7th	3.30 a.m.	Bn. detrained at BERGUES and marched to billeting Area at ZEGGERS CAPPEL	

Sheet No. 2

Army Form C. 2118.

WAR DIARY
or
INTELLIGENCE SUMMARY.
(Erase heading not required.)

Instructions regarding War Diaries and Intelligence Summaries are contained in F. S. Regs., Part II. and the Staff Manual respectively. Title pages will be prepared in manuscript.

Place	Date	Hour	Summary of Events and Information	Remarks and references to Appendices
SHEET 7 covered	Aug 1918 7th	6.30 p.m.	arriving at 6.30 p.m.	Off CAPT. J.W. WARRILOW Lt. W.H. THOMPSON. 2Lt. R.S. EVERARD. " A. WILLIAMSON " P. YOUD. " G.S. McCLYMONT. " J.P. DAVIES. " H. STEWARD
	8th	—	Day devoted to re-organisation and cleaning up. 8 Officers (as shown in margin) and 30 O.R.'s joined for duty.	
	9th	—	Day again spent in re-organisation and cleaning. A further draft of 125 O.R.'s reported for duty.	
			I.O.C. 34th Div. presented further Fench decorations to 6 O.R.'s.	Off
	10th	—	General programme of Training commenced.	do
	11th	—	Divine Service. Interior Economy.	do
	12th	—	Training continued in accordance with Programme.	
			I.O.C. 102 Bde inspected the new draft and expressed his satisfaction on the appearance of the draft. Lt. H.B. WARD joined the Bn for duty.	Off
	13th	—	102 Bde moved into the HERZEELE area. Bn moved off at 8 a.m. and arrived at 11 a.m. marching past I.O.C. 34th Div en route.	
	14th	—	Training continued in accordance with Programme.	do
	15th	6 a.m.	Bn marched to Training Area near BOIS ST ACAIRE and spent the day having during the morning the I.O.C. 34th Div and I.O.C. 102 Bde.	do

D. D. & L., London, E.C.
(A8o4) Wt. W17711M/31 750,000 5/17 Sch. 52 Forms/C2118/4

Sheet No 3.

WAR DIARY
or
INTELLIGENCE SUMMARY.
(Erase heading not required.)

Army Form C. 2118.

Place	Date Aug 1918	Hour	Summary of Events and Information	Remarks and references to Appendices
SHEET 27	15	-	Watered the Bn at work	
towns	16	-	Training continued in accordance with Programme	
Sheet 28 N.W. 17	-	Training continued in the morning. Bde Sports Meeting in the afternoon.	
	18	10.30	Bn attended 102 Bde Church Service. Bde Sports Meeting completion.	
	19	-	102 Bde moved into the PROVEN area.	
		6.20	Bn moved off and arrived at PROVEN at 11.30 a.m. and billeted in PEKIN CAMP.	
	20	-	Bn remained at PROVEN and carried out Musketry and L.G. practices on the Range.	
	21	-	The 102 Inf Bde moved forward into Divisional Reserve.	
		10.15 a.m.	Bn moved off and relieved the 1/5 YORKS and LANCS Regt in the old BRIELEN LINE (H.5.6 and d) thus becoming the Forward Bn of the Reserve Bde.	
		5.30 pm	Relief complete. Map showing disposition of Bn together with Defence Scheme appended herewith.	
	22nd	-	All quiet in our sector. Reconnoitring parties sent out to reconnoitre the forward area	
	23 -	-	as for the 22nd	
	25th	-	Bn relieved by the 1/4 CHESHIRE REGT. Relief completed 12.35 p.m.	
	26th	-	Bn moved into the Reserve area of the 102 Bde at BRAKE CAMP. A.30.C.8.4.	

WAR DIARY or INTELLIGENCE SUMMARY

Army Form C. 2118.

Sheet No. 4.

Place	Date	Hour	Summary of Events and Information	Remarks and references to Appendices
Sheets 27 & 28 N.W.	27	—	Bn. relieved by the 33rd LONDON REGT. Relief completed 8.20 p.m.	
	28	—	Bn. moved by Light Railway to LANCASTER SIDING 27/F.19.c.5.8 and marched to ROAD CAMP (27/F.25.c) arriving at 11.30 p.m.	
			The 102 Bde. moved to the CORMETTE Area.	
			The Bn. entrained at PROVEN at 10.15 a.m. and detrained at ST. OMER and 2.0 p.m. and marched into Interior Economy and cleaning up.	O.C. ? 2nd ? 2nd ?
	29	—	Morning devoted to Interior Economy and cleaning up.	
	30	—	Bn. Training in CORMETTE Area.	
	31	—	Bn. Musketry Practice in CORMETTE Range.	

Symon
Capt. for
Lt. Col.
Cdg. 1/7 Cheshire R.

Steat. No.1 Sep. 18 1/7 Cheshire Rgt Army Form C. 2118.

WAR DIARY
or
INTELLIGENCE SUMMARY. A.1187.
(Erase heading not required.)

Instructions regarding War Diaries and Intelligence Summaries are contained in F. S. Regs., Part II. and the Staff Manual respectively. Title pages will be prepared in manuscript.

Place	Date	Hour	Summary of Events and Information	Remarks and references to Appendices
ST. OMER (HAZEBROUCK SA) Sheet 28. SW 1/20000	Sept. 1st		9th battalion moved from training area CORMETTE CAMP to reserve positions in the SCHERPEN-BERG area, passing starting point at 2.29 p.m. entraining at LUMBRES at 6.30 p.m, and detraining at ABEELE at 10.30 p.m. thence proceeded by march route & new positions which were occupied at 2.30 a.m.	A.1187
	Sep 2nd		Dispositions A Coy. M.17 d., B Coy M.18 a and b, D Coy M.156, C Company in reserve at M.24 b. Reconnaissance of MONT KEMMEL and routes to the E. was carried out by officers.	1.1.187
	2/3		9th Battalion relieved 103 Inf. Bde. in right sub-sector. Relief complete by	J.1.187
		4.30 a.m.	H.Q. N.33. a. 3. 6.	1.1.187
	3/5	5-8 pm	See special narrative of operations attacked. 9th Battalion was relieved by 1/4 Batt. Royal Sussex Regt and moved into support area between V.C. RD. and SUICIDE RD. A and B Coys in front line astride Ind line between N.22 d. and N.28 c, C and D Coys in support N.22 A.4.D. & N.22. b. 8. 2.	1.1.187
	6th.		Battalion continued consolidation of new support area.	1.1.187
	7th.		Battalion relieved 1/1st Herefd Regt. and took over 1/23rd Middlesex Rgt. with new Bttn. area, then becoming front Battalion of the left B.C. Dispositions A Coy. N.23 d. 4. 6. b N.24 c. 0.9. C Coy. N.24 c. 3.9. b N.24 a. 1.6. D Coy and two platoons B Coy N.24 a. 1.6. to N.18 c. 2.9. B Coy (less 2 platoons) in reserve in entrenched area between about N.23 a.7.4. AAA?	1.1.187

(A8004) D. D. & L., London, E.C. Wt. W17711/M1431 750,000 5/17 Sch. 52 Forms/C2118/14

Army Form C. 2118.

WAR DIARY
or
INTELLIGENCE SUMMARY. XIII?

(Erase heading not required.)

Instructions regarding War Diaries and Intelligence
Summaries are contained in F. S. Regs., Part II.
and the Staff Manual respectively. Title pages
will be prepared in manuscript.

Place	Date	Hour	Summary of Events and Information	Remarks and references to Appendices
Sheet 28 SW 1/20000 1:10000 Sheet 28 SW 1:10000	Sept. 8th & 9th	9.0pm 3.0am	Bn was pushed forward into OAK TRENCH and between OAK TRENCH and FARMER TRENCH (N.23d.) (M.24a)	A.L.(?)
	9th –10th		Battalion relieved by 2nd. Batt. Loyal N. Lancs. Regt, and moved into support at P.H.? Batt. area near SCHERPENBERG (M.17.b.)	B.L.?
	10th –14th		Coy. guards on Batt. front; battalion continued very eagerly and rapidly	J.L.N.?
	15-19		all guards in Batt. front; battalion continued training and reorganization (N.16d.35)	J.L.N.?
	19-20		Batt. moved forward into support, with H.Q. at SIEGE FARM, and Coys. disposed along the KEMMEL SYSTEM, relieving the 2/4 Queen's.	J.L.N.?
	20		Working Parties on KEMMEL SYSTEM	
	20-21		Batt. relieved 1/1st. Herefords in Left Front Battalion, with H.Q. at PARRAIN FARM (N.22 d.6.1)	R.L.?
	21		Bn to withdrawn at N.26 c.7.8 and N.24 a.7.2.	N.?
	22-23		Battalion relieved by 2nd Batt. Loyal N. Lancs. Regt, and moved into support Bde. Area near SCHERPENBERG (M.17 b)	N.?

WAR DIARY
INTELLIGENCE SUMMARY.
(Erase heading not required.)

Army Form C. 2118.

Place	Date	Hour	Summary of Events and Information	Remarks and references to Appendices
Sheet 28 SW 1/20,000	1918 Sept 23		Bn. in support Bde. area - SHERPENBERG (M.17.b) - reorganizing and training.	PWR
	" 24		Do.	PWR
	" 25		Do.	PWR
	" 26		Do.	PWR
	" 27		Do.	PWR
	" 28		Bn. moved at 6.30 p.m. into KEMMEL SYSTEM occupying a position of readiness in VIERSTRAAT SWITCH between V.C. Road and LINDENHOEK X ROADS. N.27 c 9.8.	PWR
	" 29	05.30	Bn. occupied RED LINE between OUTPOST BUILDINGS (N.29 d 9.4) and OAK TRENCH (N.24 a 5.1.) HQ at ALBERTA DUGOUTS	PWR
		08.20	The 41st DIV. reported on YPRES-COMINES CANAL E. & N.E. of WYTSCHAETE and 101 & 113 Bdes. holding WYTSCHAETE wood & village. Bn. ordered to push through 101 & 113 Bde. to CANAL. General line of advance SUICIDE Rd. O.19 central, O.20 a & b, O.21 a, to OOSTTAVERNE, thence along VIERNE Rd. to JUNCTION BUILDINGS, through O.13 central to CANAL. 89th Bde. on Right - 103 Bde. on Left. Positions reached at 1 p.m. - Bn. in support P.13. 41st DIV. West of CANAL	PWR
		16.00	Bn. withdrawn to TORREKEN FARM (O.20 d.) for the night.	PWR
	" 30		At TORREKEN FARM.	PWR
	Oct 1	10.00	Bn. moved with Bde. - passing OOSTTAVERNE X Roads at 10.30 - to P.14 d 58 crossing CANAL at P.13 d 81. N. of HOUTHEM.	PWR

B. H. Hamilton Captain
Bde. 17 Bn. The Cheshire Regiment

NARRATIVE OF OPERATIONS
1/7TH CHESHIRE REGT,
SEPT. 3RD - 5TH 1918.

Reference Sheet 28 1/20000 ; Sheet 28 S.W.2. 1/10000

SEPT. 1ST. The Battalion moved from CORMETTE CAMP to Reserve Bde. position in the SCHERPENBERG.

SEPT. 2ND. Reconnaissance of MONT KEMMEL and the roads to the E. was carried out by officers; the battalion relieved the 7/O.3. of [?] Bde. in the Right Sub-sector with Batt. H.Q. at N.33.a.3.6. Relief complete 4.30 a.m. SEPT. 3RD.

SEPT. 3RD. The position of the battalion was, 'A' + 'B' Coys in front on the approximate line 300x N.W. of FRENCHMAN'S FARM to N.29.c.1.9. 'D' Coy in support about FORT VICTORIA (N.28.c.5.2) 'C' Coy in reserve at N.33.b.8.7.

During the day patrols made good the ground up to FRENCHMAN'S FM., which was, however, commanded by an enemy M.G. firing from a strong point at TANK FARM (N.19.c.8.3) The enemy continued throughout the day to harass the communications of the front line Coys. by sniping from

BEAVER ST. trenches (N.29c 6.6) 2/Lt.
G.S. McCLYMONT and three O.R. were
wounded by this sniper.

It was decided at a conference at
Bde. H.Q. held in the late afternoon, to
push forward with a view to obtaining a
footing in the SPANBROEKMOLEN ridge.
Orders were issued for A & B Coys. supported
by D, to advance, C Coy being held
in reserve.

A Coy were unable to leave their
positions owing to heavy M.G. fire.

B Coy advanced with their right platoon under 2/Lt. F YOOD, in the direction of a small copse at N.28 d. 8.1.

Heavy M.G. fire from a strong point
at N.29 c. 5.2 checked progress for a
time; then no L.G. section worked to a
flank at N.35 a. 1.9.

Further progress was impossible until
dusk. Meantime a few rifle grenades
were fired by the enemy into the copse
& five minutes afterwards a heavy
enemy barrage was put down in this
neighbourhood. B Coy supported
by D 300x in rear advanced
through the barrage. The right platoon
of B Coy, covered by the fire of their
Lewis Gun, rushed the position at N.29 c.

9⋅2, them all, to west of the Coy, followed by A & D Coys, to occupy the BEAVER ST. system of trenches in N.29.c.

Darkness prevented further progress, and the troops remained for the night along the line N.29.d.6.1 to N.29.d.0.7 with patrols pushed out in front, B with 'D in close support being on the right, and A on the left. C Coy was moved into support near N.29.c.3.6.

SEPT. 4th. At 5.30 a.m. the attack with barrage ordered in 152 BDE. Operation Order No. , and Batt. Operation Order No. 5 commenced. Advanced Batt. H.Q. were established at REGENT'S ST. DUG-OUTS.

The enemy put down a heavy barrage of gas shell on the REGENT ST. DUG-OUTS line. This made observation & control exceedingly difficult. The Coys advanced in the same relative positions, and at 8.00 had gone forward 300x where they were held up by hostile M.G's firing on them from positions on the opposite slope. Moreover the left flank was now in the air.

At dusk, however, the 1/4 CHESHIRE having prolonged the left flank, the coys. again advanced, attempting to steal forward patrols to the lip of the SPAN BROEK MOLEN crater. C & D coys led, supported by A & B. The men his reached and consolidated ons N.29.d.6.3 & N.29.d.7.7.

Sept 5/6th Relieved by 1/4 Royal Sussex.

Chmn Capt
Capt ? Cheshire Regt.

8/9/18

Army Form C. 2118.

Oct 18 / 1/7 Cheshire

WAR DIARY
or
INTELLIGENCE SUMMARY.
(Erase heading not required.)

Sheet I.

Instructions regarding War Diaries and Intelligence Summaries are contained in F. S. Regs., Part II. and the Staff Manual respectively. Title pages will be prepared in manuscript.

Place	Date	Hour	Summary of Events and Information	Remarks and references to Appendices
Sheet 28 SE	1918			
	Oct 2	06.00	Bn. moved to P.b.C.O.	
		18.00	Bn. stood-to and moved to P.7.a.8.7 (123 Bde H.Q.) to await guides from 2nd HANTS	
	Oct 3	00.01	Guides from HANTS arrived and Bn moved into line S.w of CHELUVE - Bn H.Q. at Q.2.b.6.0. (A.T.D Coys in front, B.Coy support, C.Coy Res.) in relief of 2nd HANTS. Enemy M.Gs very active.	
		19.00	Moved Bn. H.Q. to Q.3.c.2.2	
	Oct 4		Night 3/4th Enemy guns and M.Gs very active over front occupied by Bn. At dawn two wounded Germans brought into front line post, this platoon distd before being sent down.	
	5	04.00 to 06.00	Heavy enemy shelling forsa - Casualties 2 killed 3 wounded. Enemy M.G. fire active. Enemy lst day numerous strong points suspected by M.Gs. Quiet day.	
		22.00	Front extended 300y to right and posts of A.T.S.H. taken over by Rt Front Coy (A). Lt. GARDINER wounded	
	6	05.00	Heavy enemy shelling of Bn. area. Lt. Col. Mori wounded, and Capt Carcroft (Commanding C. Coy)	
		16.00 killed	Lt. Gardiner distd 9 wounds at C.C.S. RENY SIDING. Capt CDFLUNDER (commanding C)	
	7	21.00	Bn. relieved by 4th SUSSEX who also took over remainder of Bde. front - relieving 1/4 Ches. on our left and 1/1 HEREFORDS who was in support.	
	8	00.01	Bn. occupied area in P.3.6. near ZANDVOORDE	
			Bn. reorganizing and fitting.	
	9 10 11		Bn. reorganizing, training, and preparing for move to front line for attack. R.E. working parties of 100 men found daily.	
	12	18.00	Bn. left area for front line, relieving the SUSSEX (101 Bde) at 20.00 and taking over front from	

WAR DIARY or INTELLIGENCE SUMMARY

Army Form C. 2118.

Sheet II

(Erase heading not required.)

Place	Date	Hour	Summary of Events and Information	Remarks and references to Appendices
Sheet 28SE 1/20,000	1918 12 Oct	On arr	Q9c3.4 to Q10 a.01.43. B Coy on Rt, C Coy Left, A Coy Support, D Res. Bn. H.Q at Q9 a.u. (30th Div.) Go Rels - 2/Hr London Scottish on Rt.) 1/4 chess on left with 1/1 HEREFORD in reserve.	
	13	17.00 } 19.00 }	Bn. front heavily shelled - otherwise day quiet.	
		22.00	2/Lt DOME with patrol to investigate Pillbox at Q9 c.7.2. DOME missing. Patrols throughout the night failed to discover him. It was reported subsequently wounded by N.c.o. of patrol.	
	14	05.35	Attack Commenced - (will attached OPERATION ORDER No 10. Capt LEIGH (Commanding A Coy) and 2/Lt C. WINNINGTON (C Coy) and killed and C/b d/17/4/18 address Vide C/b d/17/4/18 addressed HQ 102 I/BDE 2Lt G.N. TOWNSEND (HQ 102 I/BDE) B Coy wounded	
	15			
	16	15.00	Bn. withdrawn to QUADRANT FARM Q5 a.67. (N.E of GHELUWE) to reorganise.	
	17	13.00	Bn. moved from QUADRANT FARM to JOHNSON FARM K36 a.72. reorganising.	
	18		Bn. at JOHNSON FARM reorganising + training.	
Sheet 29 1/40,000	19	07.00	Bn. moved with Bde. to Assembly Place 1000 Y E of HENIN on main COUTRAI ROAD arrived 09.00. Left 09.30 Crossed LYS at 28 SE 19.17 a.8.7. ob pontoon bridge. Bn. halted at 29 M.19.2 - arrived 11.30 Left 13.30 and proceeded through L'HUWE and PRESHOEK to AELBEKE at M 29. c.1. Put into billet in Brewery 15.30. Moved 16.15 to St ANNE - arrived with transport 17.00 and put into billets.	
	20		Day devoted to cleaning up and reorganising. Men fit except for	2.y.
	21		Warning Order to move to new area preparatory to relieving 124 Inf. Brig. 41st Div.	2.y.
	22	21.00		2.y.
	23	08.30	Bn. left St ANNE. Starting point BELDEGHEM X roads N.27. c.81. Route via rd junction N25.c.7.6. - BELLEGHEM - N29 c.03 - N35 d.0.6. Order of march B, N2, A, B6.	2.y.

Sheet IV

WAR DIARY
or
INTELLIGENCE SUMMARY.

Army Form C. 2118.

Place	Date	Hour	Summary of Events and Information	Remarks and references to Appendices
Sheet 29 1/40000	23		Bn. + M.G. – Transport	
		11.30	Bn. reached O.31.b.2.6. Men put into billets. Coy commdrs went forward to reconnoitre line.	
		16.30	Relief of 20th D.L.I. commenced	2.Y.
		20.30	Relief completed. D Coy on left, C in centre, A on right in front line. B in support. 1/1 Hertfords on left. Bn. of Royal Irish on right.	2.Y.
	24	02.30	Bn. ordered to move forward and attack enemy, & take and not move. Operation Order 265. A 23.10.18. June. 2nd Lieut Situation did not develop as outlined. Enemy 40yds to our front, 34th Div with object of gaining line of descent between advance patrols failed to reach more. 2nd Lt. Dodd killed whilst on patrol.	2.Y.
	25.		Bn. front V.24.b. & Antitypes no objectives of 34th Div. vide Bny Order No 216 & 24.10.18 attached. 102 Bny Oper. Ord. No 1 dated 24.X.18. Instructions allotted to 1/7 Horts. Indentions attach with 102 Bn. Operation Order No 19 attached	2.Y.
		03.00	Bn. attached with Bn. No Y Excent from V.24.b to V.B.d.57 C coy clearing of A & B coys reached their objective, and N.y. at Z.O.C.R.4 were unable to village of BOSSUYT D by encountered stiff opposition the enemy put down relief the company was forced into in reaching 2nd hund. Barrage of KOSB moved up to support Bn. a T.M barrage & aircraft were used to reinforce 2nd hund. Bradley Barns June & 22 O.R. B Coy was sent out to reinforce A.	
		06.00		
	26	09.00	A.1 & B Coy & 1/4 Hert attached in left. 2nd in Bn. was a coy of KOSB attached to support Bn. killed	
		15.00	D Coy crossed CANAL at link & and attained line with 1/4 Herts.	
		16.30	Bn. marched home to Biercout & now on touch with C at Biercout Lock	2.Y.
		20.00	Positions consolidated & companies deployed in depth. Harassing fire from enemy artillery all day. Bn. at Biercout Station struck several times. Relief of A & B by 1/6 Herts at Bn commenced.	2.Y.
	27	03.00	Relief completed. Bn. assembled at O.31.b.25 & billeted for remainder of night	2.Y.

WAR DIARY
or
INTELLIGENCE SUMMARY.
(Erase heading not required.)

Army Form C. 2118.

Place	Date	Hour	Summary of Events and Information	Remarks and references to Appendices
Met 29 J.49.00	27	R.S 11.50 @3.00 14.30	Brigade group ordered to move to Stt. tree in order 11 Cheshires, 1/5 Vks, 1/4 Vks Head of Bn. passed starting point N35 b 35 Bn. reached Stt. Irene & was billeted Went of Inguing a capture of 3 offs & 220.R. assembled at Bny H2	2.9.
	28		Brigade group moved to OYCHEM to form 2nd troops in order 1/4 Vks, 1/5 Vks, 11 Chs.	2.9.
	29	0.905 13.45	Bn. passed starting point Bn. reached OYCHEM & was billeted. Bde was moved in order as 28th Brigade group moved to Harlebeke in order as 28 it Bn. moved off	2.9.
	30	11.10 13.15	Arrived HARLEBEKE & was billeted Washing & cleaning Up	2.9.
	31	08.25	103 Inf Bng attacked in conjunction with 4t & french Div in Gys, 101 Brig in support — 102 Brig in reserve in its billet. L.G. training carried out. Semi clothing formed.	2.9.

2nd Nov. 1918.

Arthur Co. Captain.
Comdg 11th Bn. The Cheshire Regiment.

Unit: 1/7th Bn. The Cheshire Regt.

Summary of Operations 14-15 Oct. 1918

In accordance with your BMC65 of today's date I beg to report as follows:-

The Battn. under my command with the 2/14 London Scottish - 90th Bde. - on the right and the 1/4th Cheshires on the left attacked at 05.35 on the 14th inst. on a front extending from (Sheet 28, S.E. 1/20000) Q.9.c.5.4 to Q.9.a.6.1.

Immediately the bombardment opened my two front line companies ('B' on right and 'C' on left) and mopping up Coy. ('A') closed up as near as possible to barrage line, which they followed closely to first objective.

Over this stage of the attack most of the casualties were sustained, the majority within two or three hundred yards of the jumping off tape, caused by hostile strong points not reached by the initial bombardment.

The L.T.M's attached to the Bn. assisted with H.E. & SMOKE shell to neutralize the strong points which were too near the jumping off line to be dealt with by the artillery.

A thick fog and the smoke from the barrage made the maintenance of direction a matter of great difficulty, but notwithstanding, the front line Coys and mopping up parties kept well on to their objectives.

The first objective was reached to time and the barrage closely followed after the pause to the second (final) objective, where the front line Coys consolidated, obtained touch to the flanks, patrols from Support Company immediately being sent forward to exploit gd. to the front. At this stage of the advance the very thick fog greatly assisted a number of the enemy to escape notwithstanding the energy of the forward patrols.

On first objective being reached a report centre was established at Q.17.a.1.7. and advance Bn.H.Q. moved to FRENZY FARM about 6.30 am. where much useful work was done in collecting wandering parties of Bde. on right and a party of Div on left and sending them forward to their sector object and in collecting information from the front - also in collecting prisoners coming back in small parties - and sending them to the rear in large parties and escorts of small parties back to join the coys. in front. By the evening of day of attack patrols had been pushed up to COUCOU and beyond to WERVICQ - MENIN Railway and along to western outskirts of MENIN where they remained all night.

On the 15th inst. patrols felt their way forward still further and a Company took over posts S.E of final objective, and patrols went forward to reconnoitre crossings of LYS south of MENIN.

On the evening of the 15th the Bn. was withdrawn to the BROWN LINE into Reserve.

Casualties throughout operations :-

2 Officers	23	O.R.	Killed
1 "	81	"	Wounded
-	13	"	Missing

Prisoners approx.   200

Material captured :-
Minenwerfer. 110   M.G's 49
in addition to large quantities of rifles, equipment and ammunition.

Commanding 1/7th Bn The Cheshire Regt.

Sht 29 —¹—   Secret.
    40,000.   Copy No.

Operation Order No 19 by Captain
R.D. Thunder, Com. 1/7 W's Reg.

                    24.10.18

Para 1. 1/7 Stations will clear WOOD in
     U 18 c + d & village of BOSSUYT
     U 13 c + d.

2. The artillery programme is as
follows. At Z hour for two
minutes will bombard line –
edge of wood from U 18 c.0.5 to
U 7.c.8.2. The barrage will lift
100 yards each 3 minutes to a
line from U 24 b 25 to U 13 d 9.4 where
it will remain for half an hour.

Para 3. Two sections R.E. with rafts
& a carrying party of pioneers
(Somerset L.I.) will be in readiness
to place rafts in position on canal
when bridge-heads have been
established by attacking companies.

Para 4. D. Coy will attack along line
of canal between LOCKS 3 & 5
both inclusive, ~~at once~~ and
will establish bridge-heads
sending back to forward R.E.
dump for rafts to cross
immediately. ~~~~ The
Company will cross canal &

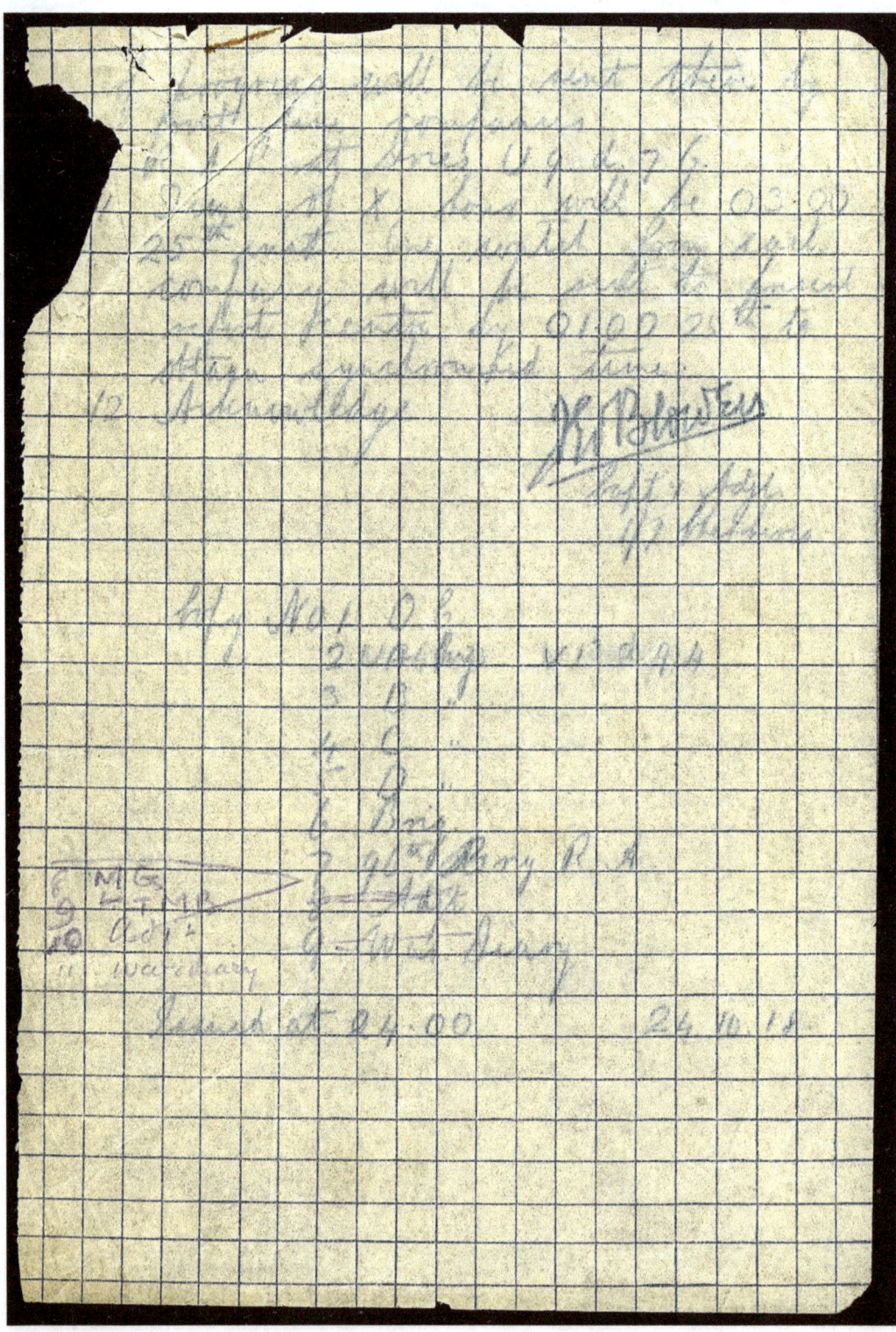

establish a line along the road
from U.12.f.9.8. S.E. to BOSSUYT.
Position of R.E. dump will be
notified later.

Para 5. A Coy on right & D. Coy on
left will follow barrage closely
through WOOD to RIVER
SCHELDT & establish line along
northern bank from U.24.b. on right
to V.13.a.5.7. on left, C. Coy
clearing up village of BOSSUYT.

6. B Coy will be in reserve & will
move at X hour to positions
vacated by A Coy.

7. M Gy & L.T.M.B's attached to
battalion carry out a programme
to be issued separately.

8. The 41st DIV. & 1/4 OXFS are
attacking east of canal in a
S.E. direction at 09.00, 25th inst.
As soon as the attacking lines
pass new front line positions
of D Coy, O.C. D Coy will swing
his left flank round to
support attack & reinforce line
if necessary.

9. Signal Officer will run a line
from present forward report centre
to POELDRIESCH U.12.c.0.0.
before X hour & will reports of

Also my Acty Adjutant Lieut C.R. MONTAGUE
I have already brought his fine bold work through
MENIN on 14th October, he being the first to enter the
town. Although he only took over the duties of
Acting Adjutant on the 20th he has been of the
greatest assistance to me. He is clearheaded,
decided & practical and under circumstances of
great danger & difficulty keeps perfectly clear & calm.
He accompanied me & together with S.O. runners &
signallers the party proceeded through MOEN and
reached U 6 d 3.6 well in advance of the rest of
the Battalion.

Lieut & QM ROTHWELL here as well as at MENIN
managed the supply & arrangements for Battn
Rations with great success. He personally
superintended the above office under heavy M.G.
& Shell fire.

22.30.
27.10.18

Lt. Col.
Officer Commanding 1/4th Cheshire Regt

Sheet 1.

WAR DIARY
or
INTELLIGENCE SUMMARY.
(Erase heading not required.)

Army Form C. 2118.

Instructions regarding War Diaries and Intelligence Summaries are contained in F. S. Regs., Part II. and the Staff Manual respectively. Title pages will be prepared in manuscript.

Place	Date	Hour	Summary of Events and Information	Remarks and references to Appendices
Sheet 29 / 40.000	1.XI.18		HARLEBEKE All Coys fired on Lewis gun range. Musketry training carried out on 30ʸ range. 100 men kitted.	2.4
	2.XI.18	18.30	E.A. dropped bombs. One NCO wounded.	2.4
			Training carried on as for previous day. Enemy shelled HARLEBEKE with H.Vs	2.4
	3.XI.18	7.30	Bn. left HARLEBEKE at head of Brigade group, marching to MOORSELE. Route :— LYS R. crossed at H.11. central — LEYHOEK — CUERNE — WATERMOLEN — road running WEST through G.24, 23 etc to MOORSELE	2.4
Sheet 28 / 40.000		11.30	Arrived MOORSELE Bn. H.2. L.23.a,b,c. Men billeted	2.4
	4.XI.18		Bn. rested in morning. Games in afternoon. # Training programme entrusted to Bay N2	7.4
	5.XI.18		Interior training carried on trying to sort matters.	
	6.XI.18		Lt. Col. Moir resumed command. Programme of training as entrusted To 102ⁿᵈ Brigade carried out. Instruction in rapid running of stations given to A. & D. Coys	7.4
	7.XI.18		Programme of training including work on Lewis gun range, Live rifle grenade work, B.7 & B.7 carried out. Rapid loading of Rifles carried out by B + C. Coys	
	8.XI.18		Brigade group proceeded to R. Coys and carried out construction of bridge & raft. Actors river.	7.4
	9.XI.18		A & D Coys inspected by C.O. Training Programme carried out.	7.4
	10.XI.18	10.30 21.00	Brigade Church Parade at L.23.c.06. Germans accepted terms of armistice.	7.4
	11.XI.18	11.00	Armistice commenced. Day declared a holiday.	7.4

Sheet II

Army Form C. 2118.

WAR DIARY
or
INTELLIGENCE SUMMARY.
(Erase heading not required.)

Instructions regarding War Diaries and Intelligence Summaries are contained in F.S. Regs, Part II. and the Staff Manual respectively. Title pages will be prepared in manuscript.

Place	Date	Hour	Summary of Events and Information	Remarks and references to Appendices
Sheet 28 1/40,000	12.XI.18	09.00	B + C Coys inspected by S.C. Programme of training carried out.	7.4.
	13.XI.18		Bn. carried out programme of training, including practice in "Platoon Syst".	7.4.
	14.XI.18		Brig. group moved to BELLEGHEM area. Bn. passed starting point Bn.g N 2. MOORSEELE at 09.07. Route WELVEGHEM - LAUWE - AELBEKE - ROLLEGHEM	7.4.
		12.35	Bn. arrived BELLEGHEM. New billets Br. N.2. N33 b 6.2.	
Tournai Sh.t 1 1/100,000	15.XI.18		Brig. group moved to CELLES. Starting point sq m in BELLEGHEM. Bn. passed at 09.01. Route COYGHEM - road through A in GAVRE - HELGHIN BRIDGE - POTTES. Bn. billeted in CELLES.	7.4.
	16.XI.18	14.00	Brig. group moved to RENAIX. Bn. passed starting point into main TOURNAI ROAD at 10.37. Route CELLES - ANSERAUT. Bn. arrived Renaix at 14.00.	7.4.
	17.XI.18	10.30	Church Parade.	7.4.
	18.XI.18		Brig. group moved to FLOBECQ - WODECQ area. Starting pt. Railway crossing 500x E. of Renaix on RENAIX - ELLESELLE Rd. Route - Renaix - ELLESELLES - FLOBECQ RD. Bn. passed starting point at 09.13. Arrived FLOBECQ at 12.00.	7.4.
	19 & 20.XI.18	09.00	Ceremonial parade. Cleaning up & Sports in afternoon.	7.4.
	20.XI.18		Ceremonial parade & close order drill. Sports in afternoon.	7.4.
	21.XI.18	10.00	Bn. bus transport inspected by B.G.C. 102 Brigade.	7.4.
	22.XI.18	09.00	Bn. paraded for route march to BOIS.	7.4.
	23.XI.18	09.00	Physical Training. Interior Economy.	7.4.

Army Form C. 2118.

Sheet III

WAR DIARY
or
INTELLIGENCE SUMMARY.
(Erase heading not required.)

Instructions regarding War Diaries and Intelligence Summaries are contained in F. S. Regs., Part II. and the Staff Manual respectively. Title pages will be prepared in manuscript.

Place	Date	Hour	Summary of Events and Information	Remarks and references to Appendices
Tonnois	24.XI.18	11.00	Brigade Church Parade.	7.4
Sheet 1	25.XI.18	09.00	Training Programme carried out.	7.4
	26.XI.18	09.00	Bn. paraded for training under C.O.	7.4
	27.XI.18		Day devoted to interior economy + cleaning	7.4
	28.XI.18	09.00	Bn. inspected by C.O.	7.4
	29.XI.18	10.30	Brigade guard inspected by G.O.C. 34th Div.	7.4
	30.XI.18	09.00	Physical Drill for one hour. Interior Economy + Cleaning Billets	7.4
			Brigade Church Parade	

H.E. Moore
Lt Col
Commanding 7th Batt. Cheshire Regt.

Army Form C. 2118.

1/7 Cheshire R[?]

WAR DIARY
or
INTELLIGENCE SUMMARY.
(Erase heading not required.)

Instructions regarding War Diaries and Intelligence Summaries are contained in F.S. Regs., Part II. and the Staff Manual respectively. Title pages will be prepared in manuscript.

Place	Date	Hour	Summary of Events and Information	Remarks and references to Appendices
Tournai 1/100,000	1.12.18	10.30	Brigade Church Parade. FLOBECQ.	7.9.
	2.12.18	9.00	Bn. route march to WODECQ.	7.9.
	3.12.18	9.30	Bn. Drill under Commanding Officer. Working party 3 offs + 100 O.Rs. on LESSINES ROAD.	7.9.
	4.12.18	9.00	Bn. route march to BOIS.	7.9.
	5.12.18	9.00	Bn. Drill under C.C. Plane table drill & ceremonial under company arrangements.	7.9.
	6.12.18	9.00	Training under company arrangements.	7.9.
	7.12.18	9.00	Bn. Drill under C.O.	7.9.
	8.12.18	10.30	Brigade Church Parade.	7.9.
	9.12.18		Bn. Route march - POITERIE - MOTTE - HURDMONT - FLOBECQ.	7.9.
	10.12.18	09.00	Bn. Drill under C.O. Preliminary inspection for medal distribution of 400 O.Rs.	7.9.
	10.12.18	09.15	Distribution of medal ribbons by G.O.C. Division. 20 offs & ORs.	7.9.
	11.12.18	11.00		7.9.
	12.12.18	09.00	Brigade troops moved to GHISLENGHIEN area. Bn. found starting point OGY at 10.00. Route OGY - LESSINES. Bn. billetted at HELLEBECQ.	7.9.
B	13.12.18	09.00	Bn. rested & cleaned up in billets.	7.9.
	14.12.18	09.20	Bn. moved with Brigade group to SOIGNIES area. Passed starting point in HELLEBECQ - SILLY - SOIGNIES LESSINES - SOIGNIES ROAD at 10.33. Route - Bn. billetted at SOIGNIES at 14.00.	7.9.
New Europe 1/250,000	15.12.18	05.00	Bn. halted. Voluntary church services held.	7.9.
	16.12.18	07.15	Brigade group moved to LAHESTRE area. Bn. passed starting point at HAUTE FOLIE cross roads at 08.33. Bn. billetted in AIN ST PAUL.	7.9.
	17.12.18	08.00	Brigade group moved to MARCHIENNE AU PONT. Arrived at MARCHIENNE at 14.00. Bn. billetted	7.9.

Sheet II

WAR DIARY
or
INTELLIGENCE SUMMARY.
(Erase heading not required.)

Army Form C. 2118.

Place	Date	Hour	Summary of Events and Information	Remarks and references to Appendices
NW Europe 1/250,000	18.12.18	09.40	Btn. continued its march to CHATELET. Route via MONCEAU SUR SAMBRE & BINCHE-CHARLEROI road. Arrived CHATELET at 13.00. Btn. billeted in BOUFFIOULX.	H.m.
	19.12.18	07.15	Btn. continued its march to FOSSE. Route via PRESLES - VITRIVAL - FOSSES roads. Arrived FOSSE at 11.50. Btn. billeted.	H.m.
	20.12.18	09.00	Cleaning up & refitting.	H.m.
	21.12.18	09.00	Cleaning up & refitting.	H.m.
	22.12.18	9.30	Voluntary Church Service.	H.m.
	23.12.18	09.00	C.O. inspected billets. Infantry training under O.C. Companies.	H.m.
	24.12.18	09.00	Bn drill under C.O. - Coy. drill under Coy Commanders	H.m.
	25.12.18 26.12.18		Holidays -	H.m. H.m.
	27.12.18	09.00	Bn Route march - with transport to Aisement and Vitrival	H.m.
	28.12.18		Interior Economy - Inspection of Kits &c. C.O. inspection of Billets	H.m.
	29.12.18	10.00	Bde Church parade in Sqr opposite Hotel de Ville	H.m.
	30.12.18	09.00	Bn. route march with transport- METTET ROAD - past ETAGE DE FOSSE and return along ST GERARD RD.	H.m.
	31.12.18	09.00	Inspection of Bn. in F.M.O. by C.O	H.m.

H.K. Harris Lieut. Colonel
Comdg. 17th = Cheshire Rgt.

Army Form C. 2118.

WAR DIARY
or
INTELLIGENCE SUMMARY.
(Erase heading not required.)

Sheet II.

Instructions regarding War Diaries and Intelligence Summaries are contained in F. S. Regs., Part II. and the Staff Manual respectively. Title pages will be prepared in manuscript.

Place	Date	Hour	Summary of Events and Information	Remarks and references to Appendices
Frévin	8.1.19	08.30	Rifles of Btn. inspected by armourer. Boys had one hours training with rifles in after inspection	F4
		14.30	Recreational training	
	9.1.19	09.30	Btn. paraded for route march accompanied by 1st line transport.	F4
		14.30	Recreational training	
	10.1.19	09.45	Btn. including transport inspected by C.O.	F4
		14.30	Recreational training	
	11.1.19		Morning devoted to interior economy, hut inspection & billet inspection under coy arrangements.	F4
		14.30	Btn. Cross country run of 3½ miles.	
	12.1.19	10.30	Voluntary C of E service in Hôtel de Ville. No engagements in Y.M.C.A.	F4
	13.1.19	09.0	Btn. route march	F4
		14.30	Recreational training	
	14.1.19	8.30	Btn. commenced tactical training by companies	F4
		9.15	Btn. paraded as though so parade for ceremonial drill under C.O.	
		14.30	Recreational training	

Army Form C.2118.

WAR DIARY
or
INTELLIGENCE SUMMARY

(Erase heading not required.)

1/7 Cheshire Regt.

Place	Date	Hour	Summary of Events and Information	Remarks and references to Appendices
TOTAL	1.1.1919	09.30	Btn. paraded for P.T, P.D & arms drill. Transport lines & vehicles inspected by Commanding Officer. Btn. billets inspected by C.O.	24.
	2.1.1919	09.00	Btn. paraded for training in accordance with programme.	24
		11.00	Lecture by Capt Dunn on "League of Nations" 30 O.R. attended. Blanket & clothing disinfected. Recreational training in afternoon.	24
	3.1.1919	09.15	Btn. route march to Short St. Laurent. Recreational training in afternoon.	24
	4.1.1919	09.00	Btn. paraded for training as per programme.	24
		14.30	Recreational training	
	5.1.1919	09.00	Ceremony as per programme. Voluntary Church service in Hôtel de Ville.	24
		14.30	Recreational training	
	6.1.1919	09.00	Btn. paraded for training as per programme	24
		14.30	Recreational training	
	7.1.1919	09.00	Btn. paraded for training as per programme	24
		11.00	he hour Btn. Drill	
		09.30	Billets inspected by C.O.	
		09.00	Lewis guns inspected by Armourers	
		14.30	Recreational training	

Army Form C. 2118.

Sheet III

WAR DIARY
or
INTELLIGENCE SUMMARY.
(Erase heading not required.)

Instructions regarding War Diaries and Intelligence Summaries are contained in F. S. Regs., Part II. and the Staff Manual respectively. Title pages will be prepared in manuscript.

Place	Date	Hour	Summary of Events and Information	Remarks and references to Appendices
Bramshott	15.1.19	09.15	Btn. drill under P.O.	J.Y.
		14.30	Recreational Training.	J.Y.
	16.1.19	10.15	Btn. inspected by G.O.C. 102 Brigade	J.Y.
		14.30	Recreational training.	
	17.1.19	10.30	Brigade Drill & march past under G.O.C. 102 Brigade	J.Y.
		14.30	Recreational training.	
	18.1.19	10.30	Medal distribution by G.O.C. 34 Division. Willits after distribution.	J.Y.
			G.O.C. inspected Btn. Willits after distribution.	
	19.1.19	14.30	Voluntary Church Parade in M.T.I. de Ville.	J.Y.
		10.30	Lecture by 2nd to attend in Demobilisation & reconstruction.	
		09.00		
		14.30	Recreational training.	
	20.1.19	09.30	Btn. rte march via Stoney de Foie.	J.Y.
		14.30	Recreational training.	
	21.1.19		Btn. cleaning at Willits & preparing for move.	J.Y.
	22.1.19	11.00	Btn. relieved by 19 st Canadian Infantry. Btn. marched to Aunslow	J.Y.
		21.00	Btn. left Aunslow.	J.Y.

Army Form C. 2118.

Sheet IV

WAR DIARY
or
INTELLIGENCE SUMMARY.
(Erase heading not required.)

Instructions regarding War Diaries and Intelligence Summaries are contained in F. S. Regs., Part II. and the Staff Manual respectively. Title pages will be prepared in manuscript.

Place	Date	Hour	Summary of Events and Information	Remarks and references to Appendices
Bude	23.1.19	10.30	Bn. stationed at Bude. Men billetted A Coy. relieved by J 26 & 29th Hampshire Infantry in the outpost line.	24
	24.1.19	—	Cleaning up & adjusting billets. C.C. visited outpost lines.	24
	25.1.19		C.C. inspected billet area.	24
	26.1.19	10.00	C. of E. Church Parade in Town University. R.C. in Parochial Church. Arrangements in Y.M.C.A.	24
			2 Coy. formed Odzyne piquet. C.C. visited outpost line until G.O.C. 102 Inf. Brigade Bn. 10th marched over A. H. Offy.	
	27.1.19	09.00	Training carried out under company commanders. Educational training & special work.	24
	28.1.19	09.00	Training as for 28th. Recreational training in afternoon	24
	29.1.19	09.00	Bn. cleaning up billets. Preparing for move.	24
	30.1.19		Relief Btn. completed by 15th A.I.F. 21st J. Bn. marched to Schonau via Hagburg arriving at 13.15. Btn. billetted, and relief of Q.3rd Hudelsher reported complete.	24

H. Knox Lieut Colonel
Cody. 1/7 Rtz. The Black Watch.

(A7092). Wt. W12839/M1393 75,00, 1/17, D. D. & L. Ltd. Forms/C.2118/14.

WAR DIARY
INTELLIGENCE SUMMARY.

Army Form C. 2118.

Vol 9

Place	Date	Hour	Summary of Events and Information	Remarks and references to Appendices
	1/2/19		Hm Battalion of Bn held by C.O. & 2nd in Command.	
	2/2/19		One platoon of "C" Coy withdrawn from ALTENRATH & billeted at LOHMAR.	
			Rest Platoons of "C" Coy.	
	3/2/19		Regt H.Q. established at LOHMAR. "C" Coy move to ALTENRATH	
	4/2/19		"A" Coy migrated by O.C. 1/4 D.Lushers. Remainder of Bn training.	
			under Coy arrangements	
	5/2/19	1300	Bn. on Ceremonial drill. Inspected by	
	6/2/19		"B" Coy attacked C.O. for Ceremonial drill Centenial.	
			...	
	7/2/19		...	
	8/2/19	1000	Coy. meet ...drill in ...	
	8/2/19	1000	Firing of ...	
	9/2/19	0930	Rout March for 6 Coys together	
	10/2/19	0930	Bn paraded for Route March under C.O.	
	11/2/19	0900	Bn paraded under C.O. for General drill	
		1105-1215	Educational Classes	
	12/2/19	1020-1200	Educational class & Specialist training	
	13/2/19	1015	Bn paraded under C.P. & Brig. Comdr.	
	14/2/19		Bn. will parade of 102 Infantry Brigade inspected by	
	15/2/19		G.O.C. 34th Division. "No Yeamates Night" Mess Dinners	
			Evening of billets & interior economy.	
	16/2/19		Day O.C. Orderly Room inspected	

Sheet II

Army Form C. 2118.

WAR DIARY
or
INTELLIGENCE SUMMARY.

(Erase heading not required.)

Instructions regarding War Diaries and Intelligence Summaries are contained in F.S. Regs., Part II. and the Staff Manual respectively. Title pages will be prepared in manuscript.

Place	Date	Hour	Summary of Events and Information	Remarks and references to Appendices
Seughny	16/2/19	10.45	Church parade for C. of E. in Prison Chapel	Sy.
	17/2/19	10.00	Boys carrying out training under Coy arrangements.	Sy.
	18/2/19	09.30 - 10.45	Coy training	Sy.
		11.15 - 12.15	Educational + Specialist training	Sy.
	19/2/19		Run parade for rank and file would 2nd in command.	Sy.
	20/2/19	09.30 - 10.45	Coy training	Sy.
		11.15 - 12.15	Educational + Specialist training	Sy.
	21/2/19	09.30 - 11.30	Training under Coy arrangements	Sy.
		11.00	Transport vehicles inspected by C.O.	Sy.
	22/2/19	09.30	Inspection of Billets by C.O.	Sy.
	23/2/19	10.00	Church parade for Coy E. in Prison Chapel	Sy.
	24/2/19	09.30 - 12.00	Coy training including musketry exercises + guards drill.	Sy.
	25/2/19	09.30 - 10.45	Training under Coy arrangements	Sy.
		11.15 - 12.15	Educational + Specialist training.	Sy.
	26/2/19		Baths allotted to Coy from 08.00 - 10.00	Sy.
	27/2/19		Communication will for all available Officers + NCOs of 60 O.R.s in C.R.E. Fatigue unit 20 O.R.s furlough on 28.2.19 received.	Sy.
		14.0.0	Warning order to move to Boulogne on 28.2.19 received.	Sy.

Sheet III Army Form C. 2118.

WAR DIARY
or
INTELLIGENCE SUMMARY.
(Erase heading not required.)

Place	Date	Hour	Summary of Events and Information	Remarks and references to Appendices
SIEGBURG	26.2.19	09.30	Battn moved Hq from prison on its march from SIEGBURG to BORNHEIM via BONN. Distance 13 miles.	
		15.30	Arrived at BORNHEIM & came under command of J.O.C. 1st Infantry Brigade, 1st Division. Bn HQrs, 'A' & 'B' Coys billetted in BORNHEIM, 'C' & 'D' Coys quartered in BRENIG.	Sy.

2.3.19

H. Mori,
Lieut-Colonel,
Commanding 1/4 Bn., The Cheshire Regt.

WAR DIARY or INTELLIGENCE SUMMARY

Army Form C. 2118.

Vol 10

Place	Date	Hour	Summary of Events and Information	Remarks and references to Appendices
Bonheim	1/3/19		Coys devoted morning to settling into billets and interior economy.	
	2/3/19	0930	'A' & 'B' Coys paraded in Cinema for Divine Service.	
		1045	'C' & 'D' do do	
			Battn forms part of 1st Brigade, 1st Division.	
		2300	Summer time came into force.	
	3/3/19	0930	Battn inspected by Commanding Officer.	
			Battn transport handed over in exchange for transport of 1st L.N.L.	
	4/3/19	0930	'C' & 'D' paraded for Coy training. 'A' Coy educational training. 'B' Coy education.	
	5/3/19	0930	Bn paraded for route march.	
	6/3/19	0930	A, C, D Coy training. 'B' Coy education.	
	7/3/19	0930	A, B Coy training. 'C' & 'D' education.	
	8/3/19	0930	Bn drill under Commanding Officer.	
	9/3/19	1035	A & B parade for Divine Service.	
		1015	'C' & 'D' do	
	10/3/19	0930	'A' Coy move into billets vacated by 1st L.N.L. 'B' 'C' 'D' Coy training. A Coy Education.	
			Draft of 7 Officers & 782 ORs arrive from 1/6th Cheshire.	

Army Form C. 2118.

Sheet II

WAR DIARY
or
INTELLIGENCE SUMMARY.

(Erase heading not required.)

Instructions regarding War Diaries and Intelligence Summaries are contained in F. S. Regs., Part II. and the Staff Manual respectively. Title pages will be prepared in manuscript.

Place	Date	Hour	Summary of Events and Information	Remarks and references to Appendices
	11/3/19	0930	Bn paraded for Route march.	Ky.
		1730	Draft from 1/5th Cheshires inspected by C.O.	Ky.
	12/3/19	0930	A & B Coy Training. C & D Coy Educational.	Ky.
	13/3/19	0930	'A' 'C' 'D' Coy Training. 'B' Coy Educational (cancelled)	Ky.
		1100	Bn inspected by G.O.C. 1st Division	
	14/3/19	0900	Draft of 20 officers & 300 ORs arrive from 7th K.S.L.I.	Ky.
		1100	Bn paraded for bathing by Coys.	
	15/3/19	0920	Draft from K.S.L.I. inspected by C.O.	Ky.
	16/3/19	1040	Bn Drill under C.O.	Ky.
			Bn parade for Divine Service in Cinema Hall.	Ky.
			Major J Richards assumes command of 'C' Coy vice Capt Leamroyd.	Ky.
			Capt Pendlebury Kerr do 'B'	Lythgoe
			Capt Johns dsw do 'D'	Ickenoth
	17/3/19	0930	'C' & 'D' Coy Training. 'A' & 'B' Coy Education	Ky.
	18/3/19	0930	Bn parade for Route march.	Ky.
	19/3/19		'A' & 'B' Coy Training. 'C' & 'D' Education.	Ky.

Army Form C. 2118.

Sheet II **WAR DIARY**
or
INTELLIGENCE SUMMARY.

(Erase heading not required.)

Instructions regarding War Diaries and Intelligence Summaries are contained in F.S. Regs., Part II. and the Staff Manual respectively. Title pages will be prepared in manuscript.

Place	Date	Hour	Summary of Events and Information	Remarks and references to Appendices
	11/3/19	0920	Bn paraded for Route March.	Ky.
		1130	Draft from 1/6th Cheshires inspected by C.O.	Ky.
	12/3/19	0930	'A' 'B' Coy Training. 'C' & 'D' Coy Educational.	Ky.
	13/3/19	0930	'A' 'C' 'D' Coy Training. 'B' Coy Educational (cancelled)	Ky.
		1100	Bn inspected by G.O.C. 1st Division. Draft of 20 Officers & 300 O.Rs arrive from 7th K.S.L.I.	
	14/3/19	0900	Bn paraded for bathing by Coys.	Ky.
		1100	Draft from 1/K.S.L.I. inspected by C.O.	Ky.
	15/3/19	0930	Bn drill under C.O.	Ky.
	16/3/19	1040	Bn parade for Divine Service in Cinema Hall. Major J. Richards assumes command of 'C' Coy vice Capt Kennerley.	Ky. Ky.
			Capt. Pendlebury Hon. do 'B'	Sy Hyn
			Capt. Johns D.W. do 'D'	Educate
	17/3/19	0930	'C' & 'D' Coy Training. 'A' & 'B' Coy Education.	Ky.
	18/3/19	0930	Bn parade for Route March	Ky.
	19/3/19		'A' 'B' Coy Training 'C' 'D' Education.	Ky.

Sheet III. **WAR DIARY** or **INTELLIGENCE SUMMARY**

Army Form C. 2118.

Place	Date	Hour	Summary of Events and Information	Remarks and references to Appendices
	20/3/19	0930	'A' 'C' 'D' Coy Training. 'B' Coy Educational Training.	Ky.
	21/3/19	0900	Bn paraded for talking by Coy.	Ky.
	22/3/19	0930	Bn Drill under C.O.	Ky.
	23/3/19	1040	Bn paraded for Divine Service in Cinema.	Ky.
	24/3/19	0920	'B' 'C' 'D' Coy Training. 'A' Coy Educational Training	Ky.
	25/3/19	0920	'A' 'B' Coy Training. 'C' 'D' Coy Educational Training	Ky.
	26/3/19	1000	'A' 'D' turned out on paper chase. 'B' 'C' Coy Education	Ky.
		0930	'B' Coy Training	Ky.
	27/3/19	0930	'A' 'D' Coy Training.	Ky.
		10-0	'B' 'C' Paper chase.	Ky.
	28/3/19	0900	Bn paraded for bathing by Coys.	Ky.
	29/3/19	0930	Strong Recoing.	Ky.
		11.30 – 12.30	Educational Training	Ky.
	30/3/19	1040	Bn paraded for Divine Service in Cinema Hall, Bonheim	Ky.
	31/3/19	0930	'C' Coy Educational Training 'A' 'B' 'D' Coy Training	Ky.
		12.30		Ky.

/signature/ Captain
Cy 1/4th Bn. The Cheshire Regt.

WAR DIARY of 2nd Eastern L.T.M.B.

Army Form C. 2118.

INTELLIGENCE SUMMARY

from 1/7/19 to 31/7/19

Place	Date	Hour	Summary of Events and Information	Remarks and references to Appendices
WEINGARTSGASSE	1/7/19	10:00	Battery moved from WEINGARTSGASSE to P.O.W. Camp WAHN.	
do	2/7/19		Lieut L.G. BUTLER M.C. assumed temporary command of Battery during the absence of Capt. G.S. DEXTER granted leave 26.6.19 to 12.7.19.	
WAHN	11/7/19	10:00	D.O.C. 2nd Eastern Eng. Bde inspected Battery and the various methods of packing guns and ammunition on limber wagons were discussed. Battery fired 15 lb Trench Practice on Live Range at DAVIDSBUSCH.	
WAHN	16/7/19	08:30	Brigade Tactical Exercise Brigade as Advanced Guard to a Division bringing out the tactical employment of 9 Stokes Guns in the attack.	
WAHN	18/7/19	00:00	Continuation of Brigade Tactical Exercise. Brigade Tactical Exercise. Battery represented enemy troops	
WAHN	29/7/19	00:00		
WAHN	26/7/19	00:00		

www.ingramcontent.com/pod-product-compliance
Lightning Source LLC
Chambersburg PA
CBHW081245170426
43191CB00037B/2047